Seasons

A Poem

A Project

And inspirational stories of faith

shared from the lives of women.

Seasons

By: Christine Heinrich

Copyright © 2015 by Christine Heinrich

Seasons

By Christine Heinrich

Printed in the United States of America

ISBN-13 978-1506197142

ISBN-10 1506197140

All rights reserved solely by the Author Christine Heinrich. The Author guarantees all contents are originally written or given permission to be written by individuals. The stories written solely by individuals contributing their stories are noted, and permission was given by these individual to list there names as Author of that particular story. This book does not infringe on the legal rights of any other person or work. No part of this book may be reproduced in any form without the permission of the Author or the contributing story tellers. Bible references are taken from the New International Version (NIV)

cgalipp@gmail.com

A special thank-you goes to all the courageous women who shared their stories in this book. I would also like to acknowledge all the many people who inspired and encouraged me to complete this work, there are so many. May God bless each and every one of you in a very special way. My hope is that these stories will help those reading to know that we are never alone and everyone, everywhere, has a story to share. May God bless you and encourage you as you read ...

Seasons, "The Project"

Ally and Annie, I love you.

You are my inspiration and may you follow your wildest dreams!

January 10, 2015

∞ Table of Contents ∞

Ecclesiastes 4:1-8................................11

Introduction..13

Seasons "The Poem"........................ 18

Section I   **Spring**................................ **23**

Chapter 1   Riley and her doors...........25

Chapter 2   Clara...................................31

Chapter 3   Thankful for the Storms....34

Chapter 4   My Christmas Present.......38

Section II   **Summer**...........................**45**

Chapter 1   Dayton..............................47

Chapter 2   Sharon..............................55

Chapter 3   That Night........................58

Chapter 4   Jack..................................65

Section III Autumn......................**73**

Chapter 1 Are you Single.......................75

Chapter 2 The Loom...................................78

Chapter 3 Ruth...81

Chapter 4   My Baby, His Baby...................87

Chapter 5 Expectations............................92

Section IV Winter...**98**

Chapter 1 Margaret...............................99

Chapter 2 Tears from Heaven...................101

Chapter 3 Listen close, you

will find wisdom 106

Chapter 4 The Gift.................................110

Section V   the Project............................**116**

Section VI Your Story.............................**117**

Ecclesiastes 4:1-8

There is an appointed time for everything,

and a time for every affair under the heavens.

A time to be born and a time to die;

A time to plant, and a time to uproot the plant.

A time to kill, and a time to heal;

A time to tear down, and a time to build.

A time to weep, and a time to laugh;

A time to mourn and a time to dance.

A time to scatter stones and a time to gather them;

A time to embrace, and a time to be far from embraces.

A time to seek, and a time to lose;

A time to keep, and a time to cast away.

A time to rend, and a time to sew;

A time to be silent, and a time to speak.

A time to love, and a time to hate;

A time of war, and a time of peace

Introduction

God has blessed me with the beautiful gift of writing poetry. I wrote my first poem at the age of 7 years old while sitting by the fire that my Daddy had so proudly made.

Have you ever looked into some burning flames?

Have you ever wondered?

Have you ever exclaimed?

That Jesus Christ is coming soon

He'll soon be here on Earth,

So say your prayers and obey your parents,

Because they gave you birth.

I remember reading my poem after I wrote it and worrying,

"Is exclaimed the right word?"

I didn't know where it came from exactly; I just wrote it down. I was scared to read my poem to adults because I feared someone would say,

"Exclaimed? That is not a word."

So, I hid it in my heart. I never told anyone about it, ever. I would write, and journal in high school when things in my life were tough. Writing is where I felt safe, protected. I was confused and lost in these years and regretfully never thought anything about saving my writing. It is now just a distant memory.

Several years later, God put poetry back in my life. I wrote all the time. I would fill journals with things God would put on my heart and short stories, but again, while these writings were logged somewhere in a notebook or the cover of a book, I hid them in my heart.

I was attending a women's retreat with the Baptist Church in a very small town in Texas. Most of the women attending were older, retired in their 60's or 70's. There were a couple women in their young 20's, and a few in their 30's-40, and this one beauty that was in her late 80's. The group was small and diverse. I had not written an actual poem, that I could remember, since that one night by the fire when I was 7 years old, but this was God's time for me to start. He woke me up far before the sun around 5:00 a.m. I journeyed out the back porch of the cabin and snuggled down in a blanket. There was one other lady up; she was in the group I will later call Winter. She bent around the corner and handed me a cup of coffee, smiled and gently said,

"I know we may all seem old to you young ones, but were all on the same journey."

She drifted off like the snow and that's when God gave me Seasons. I sat there that cool morning just writing as fast as I could. It was like He was pouring the words into me, and they were flowing out faster than I could catch them with my pen. It was fun and it was easy. It was one of those moments in life that everything felt perfect and right in my world. I was writing for the Lord and the joy and peace was un-describable.

As soon as I wrote the last word, that same sweet, beautiful lady with hair as white as the snow came back around the corner and asked,

"What are you writing?"

I said, "Will you sit with me and let me read it to you?"

She smiled warmly and snuggled down beside me on that beautiful chilly fall morning as the sun was now about to show it's warm face above the horizon. I sat there with Winter and read Seasons to her. When I was finished, she looked at me and asked,

"What are you going to do with that poem?"

"I don't know," I said, "probably nothing, why?"

She looked at me straight in the eyes and in an assertive, raspy, strong voice, she said,

"God has given you a gift and if you do not share this gift and give it back to the world, this would be a sin."

She stopped sighed and said," You have to give back what God has given to you."

I just sat there looking at her.

"Do you hear me young lady?"

That night I prayed and asked the Lord, "Lord, what do I do?" He replied,

"Write down what I put in your heart and make it plain on paper, so that a herald may run with it. Then wait, I will use it at an appointed time." Habakkuk 2:1

Seasons

Oh Sweet Spring!

You spring in the room with energy galore, leaving everyone asking;

"Can I buy some of that"?

"Can we bottle that energy"?

"If we could, we would make a fortune."

You are fresh, vibrant, full of life, and busy, very, very busy.

The world has so much for you now.

There are babies to get up with in the middle of the night, showers to plan with girlfriends, weddings to be maids of honor in, and husbands to learn how to care for, or perhaps, a husband to ask God for.

Spring, so sweet, so fresh, so quick, so fast, so Busy,

so……………………………….

Summer.

Oh sassy, sultry summer.

Your flowers are all changing from the sweet buds of spring to the beautiful blooms of summer.

You know a little more than you thought you did, would and should. You walked through some tough things and are proud to be still standing. There are still babies, or perhaps some pre-schoolars' and some pre-teens to love.

A few more laugh lines.

A couple cry lines,

but baby you still look gorgeous!

But somehow, the fresh blooms you've waited on in spring and the flowers you now marvel at in summer are growing

less and less important.

God is showing you,

growing you,

shaking you,

twisting you,

holding you,

Revealing to you the marvels and beauty of ……………………………………

Autumn.

Oh sweet, "She is how old?

She does not look it".

"I hope I'll look that good".

Autumn; Beautiful tan, brown, reds and orange.

Cool breezes early in the morning as you spend time in a loving relationship with your God

you have grown to know so intimately.

You are Autumn!

He smiles down on his creation that He has watched grow from spring to summer and now, a woman. A true woman of God;

You are Autumn.

You confidence is bold and revealing.

Your incredible fall colors are a telling sign of an incredible journey from spring to summer and here you are.

You have arrived.

You open your loving branches and welcome the birds of summer and the squirrels of spring to come and rest a while.

Oh your beauty. Spring and summer sit and dream that someday………………………………..

Winter.

BEAUTY BEYOND COMPARE!

Your white winter snow glistens with majesty.

You cover the Earth, standing tall above the
Spring, Summer and Fall, that long to have you
wrap your arms around them and hold them tight.

You speak a bit slower, and it is needed.

Your voice demands attention.

We listen a little closer......

Of all the seasons, you radiate the most beauty.

You glisten.

Your wisdom is so needed.

Your walk and relationship with the Lord
is like a lake that is frozen solid.

Spring, Summer and Autumn come and skate
across your surface, or cut a hole and go deep beneath
to fish for food and nourishment.

Oh Winter,

solid,

strong,

bold,

glistening Winter!!

Spring

Isaiah 40:31

Those who hope in the Lord will renew their strength. They will soar on wings like eagles; they will run and not grow weary, they will walk and not be faint.

Spring represents new beginnings and fresh starts. Spring is a birth of something new, or a re-birth of the soul. It is not limited to age or outer appearance, but is limitless and includes all things new. Spring is a light-hearted and fast season of things happening so quickly, if you blink you could miss them. It is that moment in summer when you turn around and ask, "Where did the spring time go?"

Spring can be a season of extreme self-absorption for women, and it needs to be because there are babies, showers, husbands, activities, school, careers and a gamut of many other things running through your life. It is a busy time. However, I encourage you to slow down and take a look around you. I encourage you to take a deep breath and pause for a moment as you read and reflect on the seasons and stories in other women's lives. There are many common denominators in all women, one being that we all experience seasons in our lives. We will all hop through a spring, walk through a summer, glide through an autumn and sit through a winter in our lives.

Several of these stories represented by spring were taken from moments when these women were young in age, fresh, vibrant, full of energy and busy. Yet, spring can also represent something new and fresh in the life of someone in their autumn or even winter season of their life. Spring not only represents an age, but an attitude or event that may be young or new. Remember, you are never too old to experience a spring.

1

Riley and her doors

    I was a Single mom and my only child, a beautiful little girl named Riley, was 7 years old. We had finally moved out of my parent's home to try and face the world on our own, it was Sweet Riley and Me! I chose an area that was very out of my means, however, the schools were the best, and I wanted this for Riley. I rented a small place in the salon that my friend owned, so I could start my own business, and found a very small one bedroom apartment that I could try to afford.

    The lack of money at times was crippling. However, my goal was to always try and make Riley feel secure and normal. I remember one month that was particularly tough. I could not pay the electricity and the lights were turned off. I went to the store and grabbed two boxes of cereal, which was about all I could afford that night, and picked up Riley from the sitters. I walked in the door with a huge smile on my face and began to light candles all over the apartment.

I told Riley with excitement in my voice, "This was a very special night because we are going to have a camp out and eat cereal, and you get to choose between lucky charms and frosted flakes."

These were two of her favorites! We played games, laughed by the candle light and ate cereal until our bellies hurt.

We shared a room and a bed in that one bedroom apartment, until I saved up enough money to buy Riley her own bed. I bought a screen which separated the kitchen from the breakfast room, and that became Sweet Riley's new bedroom. She was so excited to have her own room. One night, as I was cooking, I could hear her in this small room off the kitchen, that we called her bedroom. She was praying, "God, I am so grateful for everything that I have, but I pray one day for a bedroom with a door.-Amen"

As the months went by, I would often hear Riley praying this simple sweet prayer each and every night. I began to pray as well, "God I am so thankful for my beautiful daughter and the blessings you have given us, but could we please have a real bedroom for Riley someday with a door.

This particular day at work, had been long and tiring, I walked in the front door and had just enough time to set my purse down, when the phone rang. It was the front office of my apartment complex. They were calling me to inform me that my lease was up and along with the renewal came a substantial rent increase. I was crushed. I was barely making ends meet each month with the rent I was paying and now an increase, I knew this was just not a possibility for me. However, as always, God had other plans.

I went the next morning to talk with the apartment manager. I was able to work out a deal of doing her hair along with some of the other ladies that worked there if she would work with me on the rent. She also, had fell in love with Riley and could not resist blessing that little girl through blessing her mother.

Riley was so friendly and was always talking to people as I would tend to business coming in and out of the apartment office on occasions. I assume, at one point, she had struck up a conversation with the leasing manager and expressed to her the desire for a door to her bedroom, a real bedroom, and how she had been praying and just knew that one day God was going to bless her with a door. I had no idea that Riley had mentioned this to her, while I had also inquired about the possibility of a two bedroom apartment. However, I knew deep down that this was a pipe dream and that it would be way too expensive.

Soon after, I received a call from the apartment manager. She told me that they had a one bedroom with a study. The study was separate, very big and had double doors. "Also", she said, "we would like to offer this apartment to you at the same price you are paying now." I was in shock!

Later that month, while Riley was at school, my friends all came over and moved all of our things into the new apartment, and decorated every room. I was busy with my friends putting the finishing touches on Riley's room when I heard this tiny voice outside. "Whose house is this? "I went outside, knelt down beside Riley, so I could look at her eye to eye and hold her hand.

I said, "Riley, I've heard you praying every night in your room for a door."

"You did?" she said with a shy concerned look on her face.

"Yes, baby, and I want to take you somewhere new and show you something." I said with excitement and a giggle in my voice.

We opened the door to the new apartment and all of my friends jumped out and said, "Surprise"! Her eyes were as wide as the sun and equally as bright with shock and joy. Her smile stretched from ear to ear and completely overshadowed any other feature on her face. It was the most beautiful thing that I had ever had the pleasure to witness. She was holding my hand and squeezing so tight I thought our palms would be fused together forever, and hoping as much, as any other mother might.

We began our tour of our new home. It was a glorious moment between mother and daughter and two broken but healing souls that had gone through so much pain. Yet, God was completely healing and restoring in his own special way and timing.

"Here is the kitchen", I said.

"It's so big", she said with wonder.

"Here is the breakfast room."

"Wow, it has a window", she gasped.

"Here is the living room."

"Mommy, it has a pool view", she laughed with excitement.

"Here is the bathroom."

"Oh, my goodness, it has two sinks, and look at that tub", she laughed with a squeal!

"Here is Mommy's room."

"Mine too", she said with apprehension and question in her voice.

"Nope", I said!

Riley pauses and looks up at me a bit confused and a bit elated. The moment was filled with so much fun and anticipation I thought I might burst!

"Now, close your eyes and come with me."

"Open your……" I barely got it out when Riley interrupted me with a scream.

"Wait mom, this has two doors?"

"I know honey; it's your new room with your own bedroom doors."

She opens the doors like a princess and walks through, twirls around and looks at everything. She opens her closet, yet, another door for Riley's room. She looks up at me and has tears in her sweet little eyes.

I kneel down beside her and say, "What is it baby, what's wrong?"

She just looks back at me in silence, a tear falling down her soft peach cheek, as she turns around pointing to the doors of her new room.

"There called French doors", I tried to explain, not understanding fully what was troubling Riley.

"No, Mommy, you don't get it!"

I just look at her, patiently giving her time to explain.

"I have been praying for a door, every night, one door, one room of my very own, with just one door, and look…" she turns around again pointing to the beautiful French doors.

"When you pray, do God's work, do good things, he blesses you!"

"God did not just give me one simple door, He gave me two! God gave me two beautiful doors!"

The tears of joy just flowed down her cheeks and mine.

That night, we stayed up almost all night together looking at everything in her room, because it had been stored in boxes for such a long time. We cried, we laughed, we danced, we sang but most of all we rejoiced in the goodness and faithfulness of God.

Dear God,

Thank you for our doors!

Love,

Riley and her Mommy!

2

Clara

She jumped out of the car standing all of three feet tall, shut the door and walked up the sidewalk to school. She never once turned around to look at me or wave goodbye. Clara was in her socks with a backpack on her back, almost overshadowing her small frame and carried one shoe in each of her hands. She was mad and so was I, so off she went, just like that……………………………

It had been one of those terrible, horrible, not so good, awful, crazy, very bad mornings for this tired mommy of three young girls, all under the age of 6. We were awake, had breakfast and started our normal morning routine. Breakfast was served and we were all about to head out the door to school, when I looked down and noticed Clara.

"Clara, where are your socks?" I said, as I knelt down and faced her eye to eye.

"I don't like them; they feel funny with my shoes on." She replied, barefoot and holding her tennis shoes, one in each hand, with the worst scowl I had ever seen on her sweet little face.

Clara's blonde hair was pulled back in a bow, with every hair in place. Her school uniform shirt was neatly tucked in her skirt, as she looked back at me with her crystal blue eyes; compliments of her Daddy, into my dark brown chocolate eyes with a lazar sharp precision. I knew that it was on into battle between the two of us.

What was once, just a normal morning before school, was about to get ugly. I was ready and willing to battle, however, so was little Clara. Funny, how we all eventually meet our match and even funnier how it is usually with the ones we love the most. God sure does have a sense of humor.

Looking her square in the eyes, I firmly, slowly and sternly said, "Clara Ann Magliola, I want you to sit down, put on your socks and shoes and I want you to do it now!"

She shook her head and said, "NO!"

I quickly glanced up at the clock, picked up Courtney who was now covering herself in red marker during my distraction and noticed we had exactly three minutes to get into the car and get to school on time without, yet, another tardy.

I walked towards the door, Courtney on my hip and my oldest, Meredith, following close behind. I turned the knob and looked back, hoping, no praying, that Clara was doing exactly what had been requested of her, however, I noticed, sadly that I would be disappointed. She stood in the same place with the same look, having not moved an inch in any direction, much less, the direction that I was hoping for her to move in.

I walked out the door and said, against my better judgment, "Clara, if you do not come now, you will be here alone until I return, so I suggest you get in the car."

My patience was void, my understanding was absent and this usually loving, patient and understanding mommy of three was no-where to be found. She was absent, she was tardy, she was frustrated and she just wanted her strong willed child, who was exactly like her, to put on her socks and shoes and be compliant. This was the worst morning for our battle of the wills…………………..

So, I took a deep breath and let out a quiet giggle as I watch little Clara walk up the steps to school. She had on white ankle socks and one shoe in each hand. She walked with total confidence with that huge back pack covering her back and in she went.

The door closed behind her and she was now in the hands of someone else. I prayed that morning in my car that God would bless Clara's teacher with all of the patience and strength that I happened to be lacking momentarily. I prayed that my little Clara would have an amazing day despite the rocky start we had encountered, and most importantly, I prayed for grace and love and a much needed hug for both Clara and her tired mommy.

I grinned, let out a sigh and I drove away, knowing God loved us both very much and was on our side.

3

Thankful for the storms

     I am thankful for the storms the Lord brings into our lives, or allows into our lives. What a blessing his glorious rains can pour over and into us. He amazes me with the concern and attention to the smallest details in our lives. I am thankful that he parents us and is concerned about even the small stuff like getting enough sleep.

     Last night we all needed sleep. We were all tired and it had been a long hard, emotionally draining week. Our toddler was crying and restless throughout the entire night. My husband and I had not gotten even close to having enough sleep. There were things to discuss, things to pray about and things on our hearts and minds. Our daughter had finally fallen asleep in our bed between us, this was rare for her. She is usually a flawlessly great sleeper in her own bed. I began to have bad dreams and very broken sleep. I was experiencing what I call, "Devil Dreams". Frightening things from our past and fears kept running through my mind like a movie. I was getting anything but sleep and rest. It was around 5:30 in the morning and my oldest daughter came down to get in bed with us.

     There was one problem; the youngest was already in an already crowded bed. I picked the youngest up out of the bed, trying not to wake her and began searching for a solution, which could possibly bring one more hour of much needed sleep on a Saturday morning. At this point, I had given up any hope of maybe having 30 minutes of quite time with the Lord this morning, which was my favorite thing to do on Saturday morning.

As I carried my youngest daughter up stairs and told my oldest one to get in my bed, the youngest was of course, ready to go! "Hey" she thought, "its morning and everyone is up." She was ready to start her day.

"NOT YET I THOUGHT!"

I put her in her bed and hurried out as quickly as possible, as she cried.

"OH, big sigh"

I went back down and my oldest was now wide awake 5:30.

"This is too early", I thought.

My husband is half asleep asking in a tone not at all convincing,

"How can I help you"?

The oldest wants me to play with her. "Oh, perfect." I was just thinking before bed and feeling guilty about not spending enough one on one time with my oldest daughter. I had promised myself that I would spend some special time with her tomorrow. There had been so much going on in our lives and we needed sleep, balance, comfort, everything, help! However, I did not plan to spend this time exhausted at 5:30 in the morning on a Saturday. Then God brought our storm! Then His hand delivered our much needed blessing of extra sleep on a Saturday morning.

It began to pour, not just rain, but pour, thunder, lightning, and then bam, the electricity went out. What a blessing and unexpected blessing from God! My daughter no longer wanted to play. She quickly jumped into the bed between my husband and me. It was completely black with just the soothing sound of rain at this point. We all three quickly, peacefully drifted off to a deep sleep in God's big strong arms. We were protected by the storm. We all slept soundly, even the youngest up stairs now, for about 3 hours.

THREE HOURS!!!

I could not believe it. I could not have asked for a better, more needed gift from God on a Saturday morning. I awoke to the electricity coming back on and the sounds of birds singing after a cleansing rain. I was the first and the only one awake in the house. This is something that is not only unusual at this hour in my home, but absolutely unheard of! I seized the moment. I could not believe this was happening.

I did not know how long I had, but even 5 minutes was something that hours ago I would have not even dreamed about having. I tiptoed out of bed, grabbed my bible and hurried to my favorite spot in the breakfast room. I got my coffee, and then cuddled down on my little couch in the corner, wrapped in a blanket, sipping my hot, lightly sweet and creamy coffee. I started my bible study and spent time with the Lord.

I felt rested, loved and so taken care of. What 5 minutes would have satisfied brought almost 1 hour of pure quite time and prayer with my Father. This entire morning was nothing short of a miracle. It was at this point that I realized how much he cares for us. He loves us and is concerned with the smallest details of our lives. Sometimes bringing or allowing a storm so that our needs can be met.

As a parent, I knew that my daughters needed extra sleep to feel rested and have a good day. If I could have instantly cut out the electricity and brought thunder and rain to give her what she needed I would have done it. I would have never thought of something such as that, but our God does. He loves us and has blessings for us amidst the storms in our lives, as long as we rest in Him.

The storms in our lives are not always the problem, but our perspectives on the storms are the problems. I shudder to think of all the blessings he has had for me in my path that I have missed out on, because I was not in a close walk with Him. If I had not immediately gotten up after that storm and went and spent time with Him, I would have never seen my morning events, the storm, as a blessing from Him. I might have called it a coincidence and something I was grateful for, but would have never seen it for the true blessing that it was.

This journey we have been on, dealing with recovery, has been one wild storm. It thunders, lightning's and pours, then it may mist and someday the sun shines and warms us, but it has been a blessing. This storm has changed our lives and changed our journey. It has waked us up out of a deep sleep. The crash of the thunder has cleared our ears, so we are finally hearing the voice of the Lord.

It is a journey and we have only yet begun and I know that there will be a glorious rainbow in the end. Satan may bring storms in our lives to confuse and scare us, but our Lord allows these storms to refresh and grow us. However, for now, I rest in Jesus and I am thankful for our storm. We are finally learning to dance in the rain!!

4

My Christmas Present

My due date was Christmas day! I could not think of a better Christmas present, than to give birth on Christmas Day. Oh, how I hoped that it would truly be a Christmas baby, however, I figured it would probably land a few days before or perhaps a few days after the beloved December 25th, which would then just make it yet another birthday which was always a disappointment because it was overshadowed by Christmas. However, my due date was December 25th and I wanted to have my baby on Christmas day.

It could happen, and it would be the greatest present for Christmas that I would ever receive.

This was my third baby and I was already accustomed to the doctor visits, ultrasounds and various tests that naturally went along with a pregnancy. It was all very standard and routine, and as with my first two, I opted out of only one routine test they would want to run on me, and this was the test to check for Down syndrome.

I saw absolutely no need in having such a trivial test ran, because it would not make a difference either way how the results came back. I would never consider forgoing or stopping my pregnancy, so I thought this series of test were futile. Besides, I knew in my heart that everything was perfect with my little Christmas present growing inside my belly.

I did decide with this pregnancy, unlike my other two, to have a natural childbirth. I knew this would be my last baby and I wanted to experience a natural birth. It seemed so special, given it could actually arrive on Christmas Day, and if Mary could exercise the miracle of birth in a cold stable with no doctors or form of comfort, I could certainly attempt a natural birth in a nice comfortable hospital room, which was more like a hotel room than a hospital. I was determined and I was going to go for it.

My husband was very against me having a natural child birth. He saw no need in experiencing such pain, when medical science had come so far. I think it was hard for him to handle the thought of the pain that he knew I might have to endure with a natural birth. Men want to protect their wives and do not like standing on the sidelines feeling helpless. So, he was absolutely against my decision until the day of my delivery.

I tried on several occasions to explain to him why I wanted a natural birth and I desperately wanted his emotional support. I understand now, looking back, that this desire was placed in my heart by God for a very specific reason. I did give birth naturally, and it was horribly painful and hard, a complete battle and fight from beginning to end. This experience was a way for God to challenge me, strengthen me and prepare me for what would lie ahead of me after my sweet Christmas present would come and I had no idea the gift I was about to receive.

The birth was so painful and I wanted to give up so badly. I had to fight to be strong. I had to fight not to give up and then finally he came. My Christmas gift was opened and it was revealed immediately what was in the package.

"I have very high suspicion that he has Down Syndrome.", said the doctor.

The words rang in my ears.

"Where's my baby", I cried out.

He was taken away immediately. I could not see him, touch him, hear him or hold him. I just lay there with those words, those terribly words ringing in my ears like a deafening bell being rung by Quasimodo.

"Down Syndrome"…..Bong

"Down Syndrome"…..Bong

"Down Syndrome"…..Bong

My Christmas present was Down syndrome. I was not willing to accept or receive any of this strange news. It was just not true and I knew it!

My husband shut down immediately. He left my room along with the doctors, nurses and my sweet new baby.

I was alone!

I lay there in that bed, which suddenly felt cold and hard, staring at the ceiling, then the walls and then the ceiling again. I looked around wondering, "Where am I?", because this certainly felt like a very bad dream.

Then finally, after what seemed like an eternity, I got to hold my Christmas present. They gently placed him in my arms and I looked down to examine the gift that I had just opened. I cannot say that I did not see what they saw, but I was thinking, "I have no idea what they are talking about-he looks perfectly normal." I was in complete denial.

Then the test came back and it was confirmed. He had 3 of the 21st chromosomes, when everyone else, who was considered normal, had two. He had Down syndrome!

My Christmas present this year was a beautiful, precious, perfect baby boy with the genetic defect three chromosomes and heart problems; thrown in as a bonus. Honestly, at that time, in that room, at that moment, holding my baby, I felt a loss. I felt grief and I was scared. I was angry and I wondered, "where is he, where is my husband?" I felt so alone.

It was just My Christmas Present and I laying there grieving, when I should have been celebrating. My favorite verse began to play in my mind:

"Trust in the Lord with all of your heart

And lean not on your own understanding."

I had absolutely no understanding of why this was happening, but my only choice now would be to trust in The Lord with all of my heart, knowing that He must have a plan and He is always in control of everything. I must trust in the Lord.....

My husband did not escape. He was off in the hospital library preparing information to help and provide knowledge for his family. The kids were not around because it was flu and cold season and they were not allowed on the floor, and grandparents were lovingly caring for them, so that explained their absence.

It was exactly as it should be in that moment, God, My baby, and I. The three of us alone together coming to grips with our new adventure and working it all out together. It was going to be a wild ride and a blessing beyond my wildest dreams; however, I had to get past the shock of losing my control and facing the fears of things not going exactly as planned.

My oldest returned back to school and proudly informed the lunch lady that his baby brother had indeed arrived and was extremely special because he was born with an extra chromosome, one more than everyone else had. He was so right, looking back, about his new baby brother being very special.

He is now almost five and the light of our lives. He brings such an innocence and laughter to everyone around him. He is a reminder of joy and simplicity. He represents what we all need, because any time you are near him he reflects such joy and peace. We are so thankful for our Special Christmas Present and his extra chromosome, and I thank God for teaching us so much through him, like how to laugh, truly smile from your heart and be at peace with what life offers.

"Thank-you our Precious Christmas Gift, we love you, don't ever change a thing!"

Oh Sweet Spring!

You spring in the room with energy galore, leaving everyone asking;

"Can I buy some of that"?

"Can we bottle that energy"?

"If we could, we would make a fortune."

You are fresh, vibrant, full of life, and busy, very, very busy.

The world has so much for you now.

There are babies to get up with in the middle of the night, showers to plan with girlfriends, weddings to be maids of honor in, and husbands to learn how to care for, or perhaps, a husband to ask God for.

Spring, so sweet, so fresh, so quickly, so fast, so Busy,

so..

Summer

Proverbs 3:5

Trust in the Lord with all your heart and lean not on your own understanding.

My ideal picture of a woman in her summer season, when we are referring to life events or a time line would be someone in their mid-thirties to late forties. It is a stunning revealing of a beautiful woman coming to be truly an adult and a real life "grown-up". She is absolutely gorgeous, in her prime and starting to listen to her own true voice with confidence and acceptance of who she is becoming. There is energy mixed with an inner strength that is captivating and alluring.

There are many things to manage and attempt to control, because most women in this season, have not yet realized the liberating truth that they are truly in control of nothing and God is absolutely in control of everything, every season, every moment and every event in their lives. This discovery will come later in autumn when she has spent every last drop of energy trying to control the universe before the great, freeing, celebrated discovery of just surrendering and letting go.

Again, there can be no age of specifics put on this season. It could truly happen to a woman at any time in her life and may be something that happens over and over until the final peace of winter is allowed. Summer is a beautiful adventure, and while a bit more sustained than spring, be careful, because it goes quickly as well.

1

Dayton

    A cute little blond boy with blue eyes and freckles spattered across his small pug nose went for a ride with his daddy on the back country roads of Schulenburg, Texas. He was one of four children in his family. He had an older sister, who was in junior high, and a younger sister, in preschool. This sweet freckled nose boy was in kindergarten and his youngest brother Dayton, was only fourteen months old.

    Dayton was the fattest cutest little fourteenth month old in the whole wide world. He had blonde hair and blue eyes just like everyone in this happy little clan. His round face portrayed the perfect picture of a healthy little boy that had the whole entire world ahead of him. Dayton was a beautiful, healthy, vibrant little fourteen months old with a great family and not a care in the world, outside of when he might get to eat again to maintain his plump stature.

    They were all healthy, happy and content living on the farm in the small rural community of Schulenburg, Texas. Life was good! It was a normal day in late spring and the freckled nose kindergarten boy was along for the ride as his daddy ran his errands. It was a nice Saturday afternoon.

This freckled cutie was simply enjoying his time riding along when he looked over at his dad and asked, "Daddy, what's cancer"?

"Well, it's a disease son, why do you ask"? He was perplexed by the random question.

"Do you die from it"? The boy pressed on in curiosity.

His Dad paused, to settle the sudden strange feeling that came over him, and then replied, "Yes, sometimes you do".

He did not respond again, he simply gazed out the window looking at the beautiful country view as they rode along. Both were quite for the rest of the ride.

Fourteen months old. That was how old Dayton, the youngest of this happy family of six was when they told them he had cancer. It was merely days after the seemly normal country ride and random question had been asked by his older brother with the blond hair, freckles and cute pug nose.

Dayton had only been with his family for 14 short months when they found out the devastating news, but for his mother it had been longer. Dayton had been with her for 9 months longer. She was shocked and afraid, yet courageous and ready to battle this thing they called cancer!

It was the first week of school, and Dayton had been sick for a solid week. He would not eat and ran a fever every day. She took him to the doctor and they told her that it was just a bad cold, so she took him home. He did not improve. She went for the second visit and they told her it was a bad earache, they put him on antibiotics, and she took him home. Dayton was not getting any better, only worse.

She knew that something was wrong, really wrong. She felt it in her soul. Mother's know, somehow, they just know. Dayton had not been himself for quite some time. He wasn't destroying her office like he normally would and he just wanted to lie on the couch beside her and play with her hair. Her hair had become his security blanket. He would grab a handful of the back of her shoulder length blonde hair and hold on tight each and every time he needed comfort.

The Third doctor visit for Dayton was time for answers. Again, the doctor, who was not an alarmist, shook her head not knowing what could possibly be wrong with little Dayton. However, this time his mother was not leaving without answers. The doctor ordered full blood work and they waited. The results came back and the doctor was dumb-founded, Dayton's cells were completely out-of-whack. An ambulance was called and Dayton was sent from the doctor's office, straight to Dell hospital. Dayton's mother, Melisa, lay down beside him on the bed in the ambulance, as he held tight to the back of her hair. Her heart was pounding and her mind was blank.

"This must be a dream", was the only thought that could be found in her head.

They arrived at Dell Children's and remained in the ambulance in the parking lot of the hospital. Before they even went inside, the Doctor came out to the ambulance to greet them. She had read the reports from his blood work already and had the diagnosis.

"CANCER"!

The doctor looked at Melisa and said, "Dayton has cancer".

It was simply said, just like that, "Dayton has cancer".

"Did she hear her correctly"? She thought.

Her forehead was wrinkled with confusion and disbelief and she just stared back at her not saying anything.

"She cannot call Chad", She thought. So, someone else did the horrible task for her.

Chad received the call from a stranger. He stood there in front of his children's school in disbelief, not knowing what to do next. A friend standing beside him had to instruct him what the next step was. He was numb and paralyzed for a moment. They looked at him, putting their hands firmly on his shoulders to get his attention and said," Chad, go get your kids. Just go inside and get your kids."

The next 6 months were spent with Melisa and baby Dayton living at the hospital. Chad managed everything at work and home, while Melisa spent every night and day lying in the bed at the hospital with Dayton.

Dayton was diagnosed with AML Acute Myeloid Leukemia. This is an adult leukemia that most kids do not get and there is only a 50% survival rate.

As the days and weeks passed, Melisa found that she had to be the strong one. She could not let Dayton, Chad, or any of her other children see her cry. She had to appear fearless and courageous. However, she found herself so numb. She could not eat, she could not sleep, and she could not even feel Chad when he would touch her. She was completely numb.

Dayton became the mascot of four North, where he lived at the hospital. He was so happy and joyful. He never looked like a cancer patient. He kept all of his hair and all of his spirit and joy. He was always encouraging and brightening up the room when he entered. He was so strong, so courageous and such an inspiration to so many sick children on his floor. He would certainly be missed when he finally entered into remission and was able to leave the hospital and go home. This was one of the happiest days of his Mother's life. Dayton was home, home at last. The nightmare was over.

On June 26th, Dayton had no symptoms, no fever and no cold. However, Chad and Melisa just knew. They just knew that something was wrong. Dayton had shifted from active to wanting

Melisa to hold him all the time. He was back to holding her hair, what was left of the back of her hair. Most of it had fallen out in behind from his constant holding and twisting it in his fingers.

So, it was back to the doctor's. No wondering, no guessing, no speculating, just simply back to the doctor's. They had blood work done and then waited, and waited and waited. It seemed like an eternity, and then the doctor called. Melisa answered the phone when the call came.

She heard the doctor's voice, she said, "I do not want to talk to you."

The doctor said, "No, no Melisa, you don't"!

Melisa said, "I'm going to throw up, as she dropped the phone".

They packed everything up and began their drive back to the hospital.

The drive back to the hospital consisted of Chad screaming and crying out to God.

"Why God, Why"? He said with red swollen eyes and hands clenched like vice grips upon the steering wheel.

Melisa simply sat there quietly holding Dayton. He was not going to be placed in a car safety seat on this ride, because his safety was now in the arms of God and his sweet little hand was filled, once again with a huge lock of his mother's blonde hair just below the back of her neck. Melisa knew that she must again, be the strong one, for Chad, for Dayton and for herself at this point. She simply did not have the luxury of tears, not yet anyway. The tears would have to flow later, much later when she is awaken from this horrible nightmare she had caught herself trapped inside.

They arrived at the hospital and the nurse at the front desk asked if they would like to be placed in their favorite room. This was the room that had a huge window that overlooked the landing where the life flight helicopter sat. Dayton loved to watch the helicopter. Dayton always had a room where he could face and see the helicopter.

In the six months that they had lived at the hospital, they had never seen a helicopter covered up outside his window. The helicopter was always sitting there waiting to take flight and help the next sick child. However, on this particular day that Dayton had come out of remission and gone back into the hospital, the helicopter outside his window was completely covered. There was a special helicopter nurse named Jimmy that always rode with Dayton on his journeys through the skies to the hospital. Jimmy came in on this particular day and gave Dayton his meds himself.

The doctor pulls Melisa aside and says to her, "" Melisa, your son needs a special guardian angel 24 hours a day if he is going to survive".

Melisa looks up at the Doctor and freezes as she locks eyes and hearts with him for a moment, knowing what he is trying to tell her. She feels her heart sink as she reaches the point of surrender and possible peace with God, knowing that he will be taking away her youngest son, so much sooner than she would have ever dreamed or expected.

Melisa goes back into the room to check on Dayton. She climbs up into the bed beside him and he gently, as always, grabs the back of her hair and holds on. She rests her tired and weary head on the pillow beside him and just waits. Suddenly, she can feel his grip on her hair loosen and quickly rises up to look at Dayton. He has passed……..

The family is all in the room and gathers around to say a final prayer for Dayton. As they finish the prayer, Melisa looks out the window and notices that the helicopter has been uncovered and is flying off.

They all stay gathered around Dayton in his bed as each and every one of the family has a moment to pray and say there good byes. After the last and final prayer is said, they notice that the helicopter has returned and landed.

Melisa's dad says, you know, I think Dayton is with the angels. He has a new job now. His job is picking up sick kids and bringing them back to the hospital".

Chad smiles gently and says, "Dayton got to go to heaven in that helicopter, I just know it".

Dayton Chad Helms left his mother's loving arms entirely too soon. However, she remains amazingly strong and at peace. She does not know why God allowed this tragedy into her life, but she does make the most of each and every day that God had blessed her with. Melisa still has three children and a husband to care and love for here on earth and she know that one day all six of this happy family will be joined once again in heaven.

Melisa is amazing and walks in peace. She is an example and a light to everyone round her. I believe she was the lucky one chosen by God to bear this burden of losing a child way too soon, because he knew that she was the special person and light to handle it and bring Him glory through her strength and courage.

Melisa cut a lock of the back of her blonde shoulder length hair and places it in the casket with Dayton to keep forever. Melisa is the finest example of a Mothers love and strength in the battle of her life. There is no greater love than that of a child by its Mother and no greater loss than that of a Mother losing a child. Melisa Helms is the example of strength. Courage, grace, love, hope and inspiration that should encourage anyone of us walking through a difficult time and possibly finding ourselves questioning God or asking why?

God is forever in control and working all things out to our benefit whether we realize it at the time or not. God is in control and has a plan. If you ever find yourself doubting, ask this Mother who has experienced loss beyond all loss, and I promise you will find new strength through her story.

2

Sharon

Sharon is the sweetest little lady you will ever meet. She is older; I would refer to her safely as in the autumn season of her life. Sharon has a very small frame and stature. She wears short naturally graying hair and glasses. Her voice is quiet and slow. You must really stop and pay attention when she is speaking. She does not naturally demand attention or make it easy for you to hear her. Her spirit is quiet and gentle.

We have a Wednesday morning women's bible study in The Shop Downtown, along with a couple of art lessons during the weeknights. Sharon has begun to attend both. During study this morning she began to candidly share a story of when she was younger and going through an extremely difficult season in her life.

This is the beautiful story that Sharon told.

I was young in my early thirties and we had just moved from the city into an old farm house out in the country in Columbus, Texas. I was a stay at home mom with my two small boys Jason, who was young preschool age and Josh, a toddler. I was not very content at the time. It was a particularly rough season in my life and I was just not very happy. I had not met anyone in this small little town and had no family or friends around to speak of at all. I found myself lonely, tired and sad. This was my life as I started my morning with my sons.

I realized suddenly that Jason, my oldest, was nowhere to be found. After looking exhaustedly, I found him in the bathroom, where he was pouring my favorite and most expensive perfume into the toilet.

I am not usually a screamer, but today I became one. I yelled at Jason and whipped around in my frustration and anger to find Josh at my heels where I accidentally trampled backwards over him, making him cry. Both boys were now in tears, along with me.

I quickly and not very gently picked Josh up and held him sideways on my hips as he cried. I continued to yell at Jason as I chased him down the hallway into the living room trying to retrieve and possibly save any remains of my perfume. Just as I entered the living room, I heard a knock at the door. I could hear them clearly and as I stopped, knew that they must clearly hear me as well.

Knowing full well that I should feel ashamed and embarrassed as I approached the door, I was not. I was at the point today of reckless abandonment of all cares and concerns about impression. I didn't know anyone anyways, so I approached the door, which was already open on this cool day, leaving the barrier of only a screen to mask my behavior.

There behind the screen door stood a stranger I had never seen before. It was an older gentleman that appeared normal and very harmless. He began to tell me that his car had broken down up the road and asked if he could possibly borrow my phone to call someone for help. I didn't stop to think or discern the situation as harmful or safe; I just opened the door and welcomed him into my home. The kids continued to cry, run around the room and bounce on my furniture as he dialed his numbers and phoned for help.

After he made his calls, he sat down for a moment on my couch and I sat down as well, and began, for whatever reason, perhaps temporary insanity induce by stay at home motherhood, poured my heart out to him. He began to comfort me through his words and gentleness while giving me council in a way. The kids both calmed down and snuggled in beside me as I spoke and visited with this stranger.

The phone rang and I went out of the room to answer the call. When I came back, he was gone. I looked outside on the porch, then walked up to the road to see if he had gone back to his car, but he was nowhere and there was not a car in sight anywhere on the road. I never had the chance to thank him for the kindness this stranger shared with me that morning and the peace that he brought into my life. He was just gone. Vanished, like my bad mood.

Was he an angel? It was a very bad season. I was in a very bad place and desperately needed someone at that moment, anyone. Had God sent me an angel? I like to believe that He did.

3

That Night

It was a very cold winter's night and I was the one in charge of the carpool to take the girls and their friends to gymnastics out in the country, which was about a 45 minute drive from the house. It had been an extremely stressful day concerning My Husband. I was sitting in the car talking to his sister on the phone trying to decide if, under his current mental state and actions earlier in the day if I should even go home. I was fearful. I was extremely fearful and thought that this could be, in fact, the time that he hurt me, or really did something that could not be taken back.

The phone had peeped in several times, but I just ignored the call and kept talking to Amy. We finally ended our conversation and I checked my voice mail. It was from the Fayette county jail, asking if I would accept the charges from, "Jacob", as he said his own name in a voice that I recognized, but did not recognize. I wasn't shocked except at the shock of the relief that I felt, knowing that with his being locked up in jail, I could return to my home with my little girls and sleep peacefully without fear of him coming home in the middle of the night in a rage.

I was relieved. It had finally happened. This would be the start of my new life, my new beginning. This marked the night that everything changed in my world and would alter my life forever. This is what I will refer to as the new birth of the old me. However, the birthing process would be painful, with no epidermal and take what seemed like an Eternity, yet so worth the labor pains and the wait.

I put down the phone and got out of my car to go inside and get the girls. It was a very dark, cold, winters night and they had school tomorrow. I needed to get them home and to bed. I felt numb inside, almost like I had been put into auto pilot. I was walking, talking and taking care of business, but absolutely not driving. Someone else had to be at the wheel. I truly know this was the supernatural intervention of God. It had to be.

I couldn't have been strong enough to just carry on business as usual. I had not a tear in my eyes as I retrieved the girls and said, "come on let's go, it's late and we need to get home". My husband was in jail and my world was ripping and turning inside out, but I just kept moving forward, it was the only thing I knew how to do. I just kept moving forward.

We walked to the car, it was freezing, but I could not feel the sting from the cold. I was numb, so very, very numb. I opened the car, and everyone got in. I stuck the key into the ignition, turned it as usual, but nothing. My battery was dead. IT WAS DEAD!!!! I could not believe it, yet it was fine. It was all very well and fine. I was in a place mentally that I had not ever experienced before in my life. I was either stupid with fear and could feel nothing or so overwhelmed with peace from the Holy Spirit that I had no clue what was going down in my world and how bad it was getting and about to get in the days and months that followed.

We all got out, because I could not leave them in the car, it was literally about 20 degrees out, I walked back in and almost everyone was gone except for the receptionist and a few parents. I asked meekly and a little desperately if anyone had any jumper cables, and no one, of course, NO ONE!!!!

Well I knew someone would have to come up with some cables, because I was stuck and had no one to call. I stood there trying to stay calm for my girls. They had already had an extremely rough day from the moment they woke up and began to get ready for school.

That morning was unusually stressful. Jacob had woken up in an extremely violent and volatile mood. He was usually moody in the mornings, but this morning was different. There was something very strange going on and I knew better than to push any of his buttons. I tried my best to stay quiet and try to keep the peace.

I remember even telling my oldest daughter, not to say anything just keep quiet and stay out of Daddy's way. She was not afraid of her Father and was accustomed to an extremely close and loving relationship with him. However, even she knew that something was strangely different about him now.

I was putting her to bed the night prior and she had cried out to me asking, "Mommy, what is wrong with daddy? He is so angry, so mad, what is going on?" I didn't know how to answer her, because I was wondering and searching for the answer myself. Jacob was volatile, confused, angry, sad and very lost and out of control.

He had been through bad spells in the past and had frequently suffered from depression which he tried to manage with alcohol and prescription drugs, but this was different. This was scary and very different.

We got ready for school, as usual as we could, and he moved around as well, trying to help. He was in the kitchen with our oldest daughter, which was 10 years old at the time. It was winter and an extremely cold day. He wanted her to put on her jacket to wear to school, but she was resistant and did not want to wear the coat.

She was being difficult, which was typical, and he was getting very frustrated with her. I heard her say, "Mr. Kelley will not let me wear this jacket in class. It's very cold and he will make me take it off. I then heard Jacob scream, "You tell Mr. Kelley that if he makes you take that jacket off, then I am going to come up to that school and beat his ass!"

This was the last straw for me. I could no longer keep my mouth shut to keep the peace. I wish in retrospective that I could have, but I couldn't! I just couldn't! I hollered out to him from the bedroom, "What did you say?" In a tone that was both loud and disapproving. This was also the final straw for him, as I came to find out.

He came running into the bedroom and completely invaded my space. He pushed his face right into mine, almost touching my nose with his, I could smell the morning on his breath as he began to yell and threaten me. This had been the normal for the girls in our house lately. It was horrible, and out of control.

I, once again, out of fear, managed to keep my mouth shut. He left with the oldest and drove her to school. The youngest was not quite ready, and he would usually drive the older one, so she would not be late, and then come back for the younger, or I would drive her on my way to my work. I was walking out of the front door with our youngest, when he pulled back into the driveway, parking behind my minivan.

I cannot, as hard as I've tried, remembering what was said, or who said what first, and I guess it doesn't really matter; we were both angry and frustrated with one another. Yet, Jacob's anger was beyond his control, and had I realized, just how beyond his control it was, I would have never said, whatever it was I said, that drove him to chase me with fist raised as I fearfully and quickly jumped into my car and locked the door. He ran up to my window and banged on the class. I thought he was literally going to break his fist through the glass of my window. I was afraid, it was not dramatics. I was very, very fearful and began to think my way out of what seemed like an extremely harmful situation.

Our driveway was long and he was parked behind me, so the only thing I could think to do, to prevent him from breaking through the glass of my car window, was start my van and drive up as far as I possibly could, before I ran into the garage. Meanwhile, the little one, who is 5 years old, is sitting in the back of her daddy's pickup waiting to go to school, watching the whole event.

Jacob proceeds to get into his truck, in such a rage, I am sure he was unaware that his youngest daughter was in the back seat scared to death. He starts his truck and drives it up into the driveway behind me and runs his bumper into the back of my minivan. I scream in terror and cover my face with my hands. I begin to just pray that he retreats and backs away. I have no idea what may happen next and all I can remember is terror and fear. I cannot even begin to imagine what my little 5 year old must have been feeling.

He backs his truck up and pulls out of the driveway, what seemed like about 40 miles an hour, screeching his tires as he pulled onto the highway to take our daughter to school. I started my car with shaking hands and backed out of the driveway. I wanted to follow them to school and check on her, but I knew better than to aggravate him any further, so I did the only thing I knew to do which was something I would learn to do every day to heal and survive this terror, I drove to my shop.

This was a small little business that I owned in the little town in Texas, where we currently lived.

I drove to the shop and just sat there in my van wondering what just happened. I turned my head to open the door and proceed out, when I saw his truck coming down the street towards me. I began again to tremble in fear and quickly think about what I would do next to protect myself, thankfully he turned the corner and went the other direction, what a relief! I decided to start my van and park as close as I could to the front door of my shop, so I could get out and get in as quickly as possible.

I once again turned my head and reached to open the door, when there he was. His truck was parked about five feet from me directly facing the driver's side of my van where I was sitting. I looked at him and he looked at me and he began to laugh. He started his truck and revved his engine then came straight for me. I covered my face with my hands, shut my eyes as tight as I could and screamed, "Dear God, please save me!"

I sat there for what felt like an eternity then realized I was still alive and he had not hit into the side of my van directly where I was sitting. I slowly looked up peeking through trembling fingers and saw him fiercely back up and drive off. Hands, still trembling, I managed to start the van, tears streaming down my face and I drove directly to the police station, which was around the corner, parked my van and just sat there, wondering if I had the courage to actually go in and report that I feared my husband was going to try and kill me.

I did not; however muster the strength or the courage. I retreated as usual to my state of enabling that I would always go to, my safe place, where I knew he could change I knew he would get over this episode and straighten out, he always snapped back and what kind of wife would report her own husband, who could stoop so low.

So, I waited until I felt safe enough and felt enough time had passed and proceed on to my safe haven, My Shop, where I would put on a happy face for all who entered, smile, as I did every day, make sure everyone who entered felt great, while I was absolutely dying inside. I was so dead; I was close to flat lining. I was a fake, I was broken, I was lost, scared and knew nothing else to do, but carry on business as usual, hoping I would wake up and this would all just be a bad dream.

The day carried on and I heard nothing more from Jacob. I worked in my shop, picked up my girls after school, did homework and snack, then put everyone in the van to drive to gymnastics……..

The receptionist began to call people on the phone until she found someone who lived close by to the gymnastics facility, had jumper cables and was willing to drive up and help out this poor stranded mother. Of course, someone came and after several tries and several prayers from everyone in the van, it started!

Shouts of joy sprung out in the van, we all cheered, smiled and sighed gigantic sighs of relief. It was a beautiful distraction for me and this minor set back was nothing compared to what I was facing back at home………………

Look for part 2 of this story in the second edition of "Seasons, the Project". It is an amazing true story of God's love and redemption, and how, He is always working out what may seem like the worst of stories for His Glory and our well being and joy.

4

Jack

By: DeeAnn Hooper

"I think about Death and Heaven a lot these days, now that I'm in my thirties. "

In high school, life was easy, grades-easy, athletics-easy, friends-easy, and social life-easy. I began the notion that I was in control of everything. I still went to church sometimes, to CCD every Wednesday and I said a couple of prayers at bedtime. I graduated Salutatorian from Flatonia High School and off to college. I attended Southwestern University in Georgetown majoring in Pre-Med.

College was a blast, but being a small town naive girl with too much freedom was not so good. I partied a lot!! I started hanging with a bad crowd; I got a tattoo, started drinking a lot, and started missing my classes and not doing so well in school. And as for church, I did not go. I was spiraling out of control....and then I met Chris. He was a nice boy....a nice Christian boy. Chris was raised Baptist and was very involved in his church. At Southwestern, he was a baseball player, he was in a fraternity and he always, always followed the rules. So you could imagine, he turned me around quick...he saved me....God put him there to save me (of course I didn't know that at the time).

"But the Lord is faithful; he will strengthen you and guard you from the evil one." II Thessalonians 3:3

I got back on course...I transferred to UT Pharmacy School, he graduated from Southwestern and we got married. After I graduated, we moved to San Antonio, lived in a nice little apartment, we both worked and life was great.

But we didn't go to church, we really didn't even think about going to church. Our plan was to eventually move to a smaller town and start a family. Chris is from Wimberley, and so both of us being from small communities, we felt we wanted the same for our family. And in 1998 we moved back to my home town of Flatonia.

Naturally, we began trying to have a baby. Jackson Allen Hooper was born May 15th 2001. He was perfect and every time I looked at him, I cried. I was so happy. Well, about eight months later I got pregnant again and on September 18th 2002, William Fike Hooper was born. And he was perfect too. We were a little stressed but we were so very blessed.

"All good giving and every perfect gift is from above, coming down from the Father of lights..."James 1:17

Life happened and happened quickly. We started going to church occasionally. Jack and Will were baptized. The boys attended daycare, I worked at the Hallettsville & LaGrange hospitals and Chris continued his investment business in Schulenburg. Life was perfect...we had a perfect little family, and everything seemed to be under my control.

Until.....

Saturday, April 2nd, Jack had opening ceremonies and his first baseball game. Sunday, we went to 7:30 church, Chris and the boys played catch, shot the bow and arrow and had a nice day together while I was at work. That evening Jack started running fever. We gave him ibuprofen and he went to bed.

In the middle of the night he threw up twice...I gave him a Phenergan and he slept the rest of the night (thinking it was a 24 hour stomach bug). The next day, which was Monday, my Dad stayed with him in the morning (Chris & I had to work).

Jack had high fevers, in which we were alternating ibuprofen and Tylenol...which kept the fever down...and he also complained about the heal of his foot hurting (the foot had no bruising, swelling or cut) so Dad started soaking his foot in Epson salt. Jack said that is was better.

My Mom took over later that afternoon and she continued the ibuprofen with cold rags and finally the fever broke at about 3 PM. Jack did his homework and when Chris got home they ate dinner and did the night time routine. When I got home, Jack was in our bed downstairs and I went to him and asked him how he felt and he said ok. He definitely wasn't back to himself...very lethargic.

I asked if his head hurt or stomach hurt and he said no, but he did complain about his foot. I looked at it...didn't see anything wrong (I thought that I would take him to the doctor the next day to at least maybe x-ray his foot). I said. Let's put pillows under it to elevate it...so I did and he said that it was better.

We said our good nights and he went to sleep. Since he was sleeping in our bed, I slept on the couch. At about midnight, Jack woke me up and asked if he could have cereal in the morning and I said sure and then a little while later he asked if he could have cereal now...so I got up and got him a bowl of cereal (with milk) and he ate the whole bowl (I thought he was feeling better).

I had lain back down and I heard him put the bowl in the sink and lay down on the love seat next to me. A little later, I heard him get up and get some water and then a little while later Chris wakes me up. He said that Jack laid back in bed with him and it woke him up, Chris felt Jack and he was cold...Chris put on the light and Jack's face had little reddish-brown freckles all over it and his lips were blue.

When I saw this I immediately got dressed and took him to the emergency room (before we went I took his temp and it said 92). On the way to the ER Jack complained about his stomach hurting...he said he drank too much water and he was trying to make himself throw up. We got to the ER at about 3:30 AM Tuesday morning and we walked in and the nurse took his temperature and it was unreadable.

I asked why it would it be so low and he said that maybe it was sepsis (infection in the blood). They started IV fluids, antibiotics, Jack was very restless and apparently hurting all over at this point, they were trying to draw blood and his heart rate was high and his breathing was short. They decided to call Life-Flight (to take him to Dell's Children's) and they were on there way.

At some point Jack said that he was going to die and I reassured him that he would not twice and then he said "I'm going to miss you Mom" and a short time later he started to roll his eyes back, but before that... he looked straight in my eyes and gave me the biggest smile...at the time I thought it was very strange but looking back on it, it was God.

They then incubated him (so he could breathe) and shortly after he had a heart attack. They got him back and the helicopter landed. Chris finally got there with Will, my Dad got there to pick Will up and we were planning on going with Jack in the helicopter. Before Life-Flight could take him, he arrested again and they never got him back. The team continued to do CPR. We were in total shock, we kept praying and praying, through the course of the morning I said the Hail Mary repeatedly.

After a while, the doctor called it...."Jack was gone".

Chris became angry and started punching the air; I thought I was in a dream "I was definitely not in control". Father Tim was called and he came and gave Jack, the anointing of the sick. The Justice of the Peace ordered an autopsy. It took 2 months to get the autopsy back in which it concluded the cause of death was a viral-like syndrome of unknown origin. So basically, no one knows....I took it as God's Will.

But I still had a hard time with the outcome. I blamed myself, I resented my parents, I couldn't eat or sleep, I was loosing my hair and I was experiencing dizzy spells due to stress. I cried everyday for about 8 months. I got some peace of mind when I had a local physician read the autopsy report and ER record...he reassured me that we did all the right things...some things just happen. I also felt comfort when he expressed his faith in God and that one day we will understand.

It makes me so sad when I think of all the people that didn't get to meet Jack or get to know him. My husband wrote Jack's eulogy and I would like to share a little of it with you.

Jackson Allan Hooper was born on May 15th, 2001. Most people called him Jack. We affectionately called him Jackie.

"Many of you were familiar with Jack, but many did not truly know who he was."

At school, maybe he was the classmate who wanted to talk continuously about his favorite video games or talk to him-self on the playground at recess. Perhaps he was the student in the hallway who appeared to be in his own world, at times paying little attention to his surroundings.

At church, he may have been the little boy who said "bless you" too loudly during a moment of silence or wanted to extend a handshake of peace even though you were two rows away. But Jackie knows God and never fussed or complained about going to church. Now that I think about it, I'm sure he saw it as another opportunity to see Mrs. Marburger and eat at McDonald's.

Around town, he could have been the boy at the hardware store who, for some unknown reason, was playing with the toilet plungers. But you always told him hello & attempted to have a conversation with him no matter how awkward it may have been.

At the grocery store, he may have recognized your face, walked up and said, "Do I know you?" Or maybe he was running down one of the isles, holding up a huge can saying, "Look Dad, its Popeye Spinach." Thanks to Jack, I know first hand that Popeye Spinach is sold at grocery stores throughout Texas, New Mexico, Colorado & even Florida.

On the football field & the baseball diamond, he was the player who didn't seem to have much natural talent & had a difficult time understanding the instructions to the exercise that his teammates seemed to complete with ease. I never faulted him for his lack of ability but at times became frustrated with his effort for which he would always over-apologize & correct.

During the scout meetings, he may have starred off while his mind re-played episodes of Sonic the Hedgehog or some other cartoon that captivated his attention, when he should have been focused on his leader.

Obviously, Jack was a little different. Family & friends would often say things like, "That's just Jack" or ask the question, "what do you expect, it's Jack?" How else would you explain a child who wanted to eat ice out of a drink cooler while standing in line at a local restaurant? Or one of my personal favorites, run his hands over every package of frozen meat at the grocery store and then lick his fingers.

He tried to pee in public, he licked the gymnasium floor & and he laid face down, spread eagle, on a bench in the Wal-mart Customer Service area with Will on top of him while Jack rubbed his face from side to side on the bench cushion. I can only imagine what the 20 people standing in the return line must have thought. I'll admit, I did chuckle for a second as I watched from a distance.

I love sharing this with people because it is a true depiction of Jack and gives you a glimpse of Jack's beautiful soul.

I have always been thankful for each and every day because I am a realist and I always have been….I know, we all die. I was committed to teaching my children to KNOW God because one day I would die and they wouldn't have me to lead them or help them. But I never fathomed that my children could die before me. I remember telling my first grade CCD kids, that same fact, they would all be a little shocked but I would reassure them that they would live long, long lives before they die. But will they? We have to prepare our children. WE ARE NOT IN CONTROL!!!

"God is the only constant in our lives…..this is huge. God is our only constant…..we can lose jobs, lose money, lose friends, lose parents, lose spouses and even lose Children. And when we die, we die alone…unless you KNOW God…. God stays!!!!!!"

Authored By:

DeeAnn Hooper

Jack's legacy lives on, please visit:

turtlewingfoundation.org

Oh sassy, sultry summer.

Your flowers are all changing from the sweet buds of spring

to the beautiful blooms of summer.

You know a little more than you thought you did,

would and should.

You walked through some tough things

and are proud to be still standing.

There are still babies,

or perhaps some pre-schoolers and some pre-teens to love.

A few more laugh lines.

A couple cry lines, but baby you still look gorgeous!

But somehow, the fresh blooms you've waited on in spring and

the flowers you now marvel at in summer

are growing less and less important.

God is showing you,

growing you,

shaking you,

twisting you,

holding you,

Revealing to you the marvels and beauty of ....

Autumn

Philippians 4:4-7

Rejoice in the Lord always, I will say it again: Rejoice! Let your gentleness be evident to all. The Lord is near. Do not be anxious about anything, but in every situation, by prayer and petition, with Thanksgiving, present your request to God. And the peace of God, which transcends all understanding, will guard your hearts and your minds in Christ Jesus.

What mature women want is this: the light heartiness of our youth with the added depth our suffering of the past has given us. Through the grace of God, it is within our grasp to have both. This is what we hope to experience as we enter autumn!

Genuine spiritual experience transforms our suffering into something beautiful and lifts the heavy burdens from our hearts. The older we get, the lighter we can become, if we will allow ourselves the freedom. It takes effort to move in this direction, because it can seem counter to the way that the world has taught us.

However, moving counter to the ways of the world should be the purpose of our lives. This is where the freedom that comes through each season is experienced. So, don't get stuck on a certain season. Sometimes, just move counter and see someone in there winter behaving like spring….it is so refreshing.

1

"Are you Single?"

"Are you single?" she said in a raspy, strong voice.

"Excuse me?" I thought, "Who are you?"

I turned around in my chair and there stood Dorothy. She was a large woman with short gray hair and two chins. Her forward questions still lingered in her bright sparkling eyes. I did not want to answer what I thought to be a rude and forward question.

"Who are you and why do you care? "I thought.

However, "Yes, um yes I am." I shuddered

Dorothy's large face lit up as she slapped her thigh in excitement.

"Great, I have just the person for you."

I stood up hoping to find some way out of this uncomfortable situation and I was stopped again by Dorothy.

"Oh my goodness, your short too, oh this is perfect. It is absolutely perfect."

I was convinced at this point that this lady had lost her mind. How do I get away without hurting Mary's feelings? Mary is so sweet and has been asking me over for tea since I moved in here 2 months ago, but this Dorothy, this I cannot handle.

"Short?"

The one word question was all I could get out when Dorothy, once again, interrupted me.

"There is this new guy in the neighborhood, his name is Gary. He is handsome, very smart, very single and short. Yep, you two are perfect!"

My face must have turned three shades that evening. I am sure I could have given the sunset a run for its money. I could feel my ears burning and my stomach was suddenly tangled in knots. I suddenly felt speechless, which was not at all true to my character. I just wanted to run away.

"You may not know this Dorothy, but I am recently widowed and not at all wanting to meet someone."

"Well think about it." Dorothy said smiling.

My Frankie was a wonderful man, my rock and my strength. We had shared 46 wonderful years together and raised two beautiful daughters and 5 amazing grandchildren. The thought of ever spending time with any other man, even in friendship was so far from my mind, it could not have even been considered a seed.

This seed was not going to be planted. I assure you of that fact. This season is so new to me now and this Dorothy, this people gardener planting her seeds, just made me feel irritated and tense. I wondered if she could feel the burn I felt or hear my heartbeat as I could.

"Thank you Dorothy, but no thank you." I said as politely as I could.

"I have to get out of here." I thought.

I turned to Mary, who had an expression on her face that read I'm sorry. I quickly blurted out the first lie I could get out of my mouth, "I Forgot I left a pie in the oven. I must get home before we smell burnt cherries all the way down here in your yard."

Then I ran. I ran home up the hill out of breath through my front door and just stopped as my weaving loom just sat there in the living room staring at me with disapproval. I walked over to the loom, looked up at the last picture we had all taken together before he died hanging on the wall above my beautiful loom.

I collapsed on the small rectangular bench and melted in a pool of tears, sobs and total heartbreak. This new season the Lord had brought me was unwelcome and I was so angry with my constantly unanswered question of why. We just were getting settled into our retirement. I was claiming my autumn season with proud excitement and anticipation and now this.

This Dorothy gardener wanting to plant seeds in my head about some handsome older man named Gary that was short and perfect for me? No, I had perfect and I am not going to replace it. Oh, hickory Hills retirement village. What am I doing here? I held on to the loom for dear life and drifted off to the memories of it's coming into my life and how my Frankie had hated the idea of this loom.

2

The Loom

"It cost how much?", he said with shook and total disapproval all rolled up into one sentence.

"Frankie, it would be so relaxing for me to be able to weave right here in our home. The center is so far for travel, and I could get so much done here." Doris replied as she gently snuggled up to him and nibbled on his ear.

Doris, knew one way to always gain the approval of Frankie, was to work her women's charming magic. She slipped on her cutest nightgown and freshened up her face. Doris nestled into bed and pretended to be reading until Frankie came in the room. She could see his glare over on her out of the corner of her eye and could not help but give a little grin as if she was reading something humorous.

Frankie and Doris both knew what was about to happen and that Doris would in fact get her precious loom. She loved her husband that night like she was weaving at the foot of her loom, gently and softly. The rhythm that transpired that night reminded her of the heartbeat of her loom as she pushed the petal up and down as the yarn gently weaved in and out creates her masterpiece.

Frankie and Doris were a masterpiece. They met when they were very young and Doris always knew that God had placed them in one another's life. After 25 years of marriage, they could complete one another's sentences, even when they wanted to change them, like Frankie wanting to change Doris's mind about getting the $3000.00 weaving loom. However, no price was ever to large in exchange for Frankie seeing Doris smile that crocked little smile that He loved to provoke, however, absurd or expensive.

Frankie would now be the proud co-owner of a very large weaving Loom that would greet him every day. He loved that loom that would greet him every evening when he walked in the door from work. Frankie had no idea how much he would grow to appreciate that loom, and he did. He absolutely adored it.

Frankie would come home after a long day, exhausted and tired and open the front door to their living room and there would be Doris. The stereo would be playing loudly and wonderful smells would be drifting from the kitchen reminding him of how hungry he was and how happy he was to be home and end his day. Frankie's eyes would drift over to find Doris', back facing him, gently moving in a rhythm on her loom.

She would be lost in the art of weaving rocking back and forth and singing out along with the stereo. He loved it and he loved Doris. She was so beautiful, just sitting straight up on that small wooden bench in her long flowing summer skirt pulled up above her knees and her cool little tank top.

Frankie would stand there and quietly watch for as long as he could before Doris would since his presence spiritually and gently turn around with a little smile and say, "Hi Honey, how was your day?" Cute, Doris was just beautiful and cute and Frankie loved her and loved that crazy loom.

3

Ruth

Ruth is a light, a true light. Her smile is bright and warm and makes you feel the urge to reach out and hug her. She is a middle aged beautiful Hispanic lady. Her small brown eyes sit just above her cheek bones and warm brown skin, which surrounds the sweetest smile you will ever have the pleasure to see. The best word to describe Ruth is cute. Ruth is a cutie.

She works at the dentist office around the corner from my coffee shop and comes in frequently, always wearing her cute, comfy scrubs, tennis shoes and her endearing smile. Her Hair is black and usually loosely pulled back or piled up on her head. She does not wear much makeup and does not need it. Her complexion is flawless, along with her personality. You cannot, not love Ruth. Ruth is one of those people that if you do not like them, than chances are, there is something very, terribly wrong with you.

The first time I met Ruth was when she came in to order a coffee and ask if she could leave a donation jar and a flyer to collect money for her sick Granddaughter. Her oldest son's daughter, who was only 7 years old, was suffering from cancer and the medical bills were piling up.

I could see the sadness in her eyes, but I could also see her strength and was amazed at her strong, positive outlook. Ruth was not a victim and she did not believe her sweet little granddaughter to be a victim either. She just wanted to see her healed, if this was God's will.

I asked Ruth a couple of years later to share her wonderful story, and this is what she wrote:

Where do I begin? It all began on July 12, 2008, when I heard the terrifying news that my 7 year old granddaughter Hailey had an inoperable brain tumor.

" What does that mean", I thought!

"Is she going to be alright?"

"What can be done to fix this, and when?" my mind raced with questions, to the point of exhaustion.

I quickly set off for the hospital. I slowly walked into the room where they had Hailey waiting as they prepared her for more test, and she called out to me.

"Grandma", she said in a sweet voice. I noticed, as I walked closer that Hailey was wearing glasses. This was the first time I had ever seen her wear glasses. She looked different to me, but nothing could hide the beauty of her pureness and innocence that shined through her loving eyes.

My granddaughter was the most beautiful sight that I had ever seen. Hailey was a light, a true light. I turned and notice my son and daughter in law sitting in the corner of the room with a horrible look of un-belief, confusion and pain that I had never seen before.

"Why, why is this happening? Where did we go wrong?" my son cried out as he jumped up and crossed the room to embrace me with warm tears falling on my shoulder. No, it's not what we did wrong, it's what do we need to do right? Right now, what do we do?" My daughter in-law said, correcting my son's outburst.

She had now taken control of all of Hailey's medical decisions and the situation, because my son had completely checked out. She had no choice she had to be the strong one. She had to draw the strength to fight, for Hailey. We all did!

God quickly became the target of all of my son's blame.

"Why is God doing this to my daughter?" he would too often ask me.

"She's my little girl; she has never done anything to anyone." He cried out in frustration.

God was to blame and He checked God out of the hope for a possible solution completely. Prayer was no longer to be allowed in his presence. God was no longer allowed to be spoken of in their home.

One weekend on one of my usual visits, I sat beside Hailey stroking her soft brown hair that was tucked behind her cute little glasses as she sat on the bed beside me.

"Do you believe in God, Hailey?" I asked.

"Of course, I do Grandma." she responded quickly and cheerfully.

"Why do you ask?" she said.

"Oh, sweetie, just because I know that He loves you very, very much."

My heart was warmed and content with her response.

As the months went by, Hailey is spared all the results of her condition as she undergoes several rounds of Chemo and radiation. Despite her frail little body and obvious outward signs of the toll that all the chemicals were taking on her physically, Hailey stays amazing bright, cheerful and a positive light to all around her.

Her Mama begins to worry and fret about her little girl losing her hair and doesn't want her to experience the pain of feeling different from everyone, so she decides to shave her own head, but to her amazement, Hailey never lost her hair and continued to wear her purple highlights in her long dark brown hair, throughout all of her treatments.

Every day I would pray the same simple prayer for Hailey.

"God, please do not take Hailey to be with you. Heal her; remove this awful tumor from her head. God, you can do this, and I receive it with open arms. Please hear my prayer God, in Jesus name I pray."

As months pass, Hailey is not showing any signs of improvement. However, I still pray consistently, never missing a day, minute or second of thought or prayer for my precious granddaughter's healing. We are all pulling together and doing everything we can to make any and all of Hailey's dreams come true. Most of them were a success, but the dream of her surviving cancer was something that was all out of our control and in the hands of God.

Hailey enjoys spending most of her time, which was reserved to a bed or chair, drawing and writing messages to her family. Hailey seemed to have an insight that many of the adults in her life were lacking, a faith that surpassed all understanding for a little girl of her young age.

One day, she calls her family into the room and asks us all to sit down, because she has something that she needs to tell us and she wants us to hear her and listen very closely.

Once Hailey has our full attention, she starts.

"Mommy, Daddy, Grandma, I know that when I go to be with God, I am going to be alright. I do not want you to worry about me. I love you all very, very much and want to thank you for loving me and taking such good care of me. I know that you have all done all that you could do for me."

I wish that this story had an ending, but this is a story in progress. Hailey went home to be with her Heavenly Father on February 9 2009 at 1:31 a.m. Some may be tempted to assume that my prayers did not get answered. No, they did not, not the way that I would have like them to have been answered, but then again, maybe they did get answered after all.

Hailey is healed, her tumor is gone and God did remove it and I receive her healing with open arms. My Hailey is with God, which is a far better place to be than any of us here on earth could imagine. So yes, my prayers were all answered!

We had Hailey to love for 7 years, 7 months, 22 days, 1 hour and 31 minutes. I am thankful down to the seconds. We are never promised or guaranteed tomorrow. We only have this moment. We are all passing thru, some longer than others and all for a certain purpose in God's time. However, it is how we use our time while we are passing through that matters more than how long our passing through may last.

My granddaughter passed through in what I feel is far too short of time, but her impact will be forever felt. She passed with total and complete love in her heart and wisdom far beyond her 7 years. Hailey lived her life to the fullest, without a single regret. She is now at her final destination. Why did God choose this path for her departure? I do not know, but I do know, it's not how we leave, but were we go.

I will continue to pray for my son and daughter and law to allow God back into their lives and home, and I believe that God has a plan. So, I will continue to pray………………………

Dearest Hailey,

Until we are together again!

Love,

Grandma Ruthie

4

My Baby, His Baby

By: Emily Neal

Funny how our lives and trials mimic Christ's love and lessons for us over and over. Not that anything I walk through is a fragment of what Christ did for us on that cross but He is always teaching us through His walk. Christ's life, the greatest love story ever told. Love, wow what a word, such a beautiful thing. Doesn't seem like love should be a hard thing since it's all about beauty, forgiveness and grace. Yet it is sometimes the hardest thing we ever learn to do.

When I became a parent I think I truly knew love in a deeper way. This little baby, little creation, this blessing that you wait and prepare or at least think you prepare for but yet once it arrives completely change your world. You are so completely consumed by this love that has now been magnified times a gazillion! What a love affair. This little baby, this little creation you created and are now responsible for. Their every existence, their every need is dependent on you.

One of the hardest lessons I've ever had to learn was that after God gave me this child, His child I would have to give him back? This child, my baby, His baby the one I waited on...the one I nurtured...the one I poured myself into....I have to give back? Wait a minute, I'm a Mother.....this is my job.....the job you gave me to do.....You gave me this child and now Your telling me "Thanks, but you have to give him to me now? That I have to Trust You?

Wait a minute; it's been 18 years that I have poured into his life, this child, my baby! Wait a minute.....I've loved him...I've nurtured him... I cared for him......didn't I do it right?

No one really warns you about the rebellion...about the battles.......about the sleepless nights of warfare. Oh sure you read Proverbs after they are born that tells us to raise up a child....and think I'm going to be a great Christian parent! I was in church every time the door opened. I made sure they were at every church camp and young life camp. We did all the right things, we spoke all the right words, and we believed the best for them.

Somehow we think as we watch 'other' parents kids walking in rebellion that it won't happen to our child after all we are 'youth pastors' we are 'foster parents'. We've been taking over 50 hours of training a year to learn how to do this parenting thing. We love our kids...they are our priority....WE GOT THIS!

Then one day it happens...you start seeing the signs. You know 'all' the kids drink but you still don't want to think it's yours. You confront them and they deny it and somehow convince you they are different. You want to believe them because maybe the truth would be too hard. So we continue praying and hoping it's not too bad. Then you see signs of moodiness, hoping it's just puberty not drugs like the commercial says?

One day as I was cleaning house listening to T.D. Jakes he spoke out "Woman, the enemy doesn't want you; he wants your first born!" It pierced my spirit to the deepest most inner part, but I still did not realize the call on my son's life at that point. I just wanted him to be ok...to be safe...to not do drugs. I had no idea the Lord would take my baby, His baby and turn him into someone on fire and passionate about God!

God brought someone into our life who shared the story of his son and his venture into drugs. He was a wonderfully courageous man of God. At that point we still weren't sure but thought why not drug test him after all if this man's son could go through something like this is it possible our son could?

The drug test was positive for marijuana. Ok we can deal w/this after all he said he won't do it again! Some time passed and the Lord spoke to my spirit and said 'cocaine'. I just knew there was no way he could do that he doesn't even have money and no one does that here? We once again did the drug test. He tested positive again for marijuana. He looked relieved and my husband took him to school. I still kept thinking cocaine.

As I went to look one more time, there it was 'cocaine'. Our deepest fear...our baby, my baby that God gave us, that we raised in church that we taught the word of God too...was doing drugs. This child, my baby, His baby, He gave "me" to care for, was walking in rebellion, was walking in darkness, was walking out the door and away from us.

I have never felt such sadness, such darkness such loneliness ever. Just as Christ gave His all on that cross and sacrificed everything for us, for me, for my baby...His baby....sin enters in and the tables turn and we walk away from Him. Just as the table turned on us and my baby, His baby walked away from us. He left home. I felt robbed and I was! The enemy stole my child, stole his senior year, stole his joy, and stole his strength.

Once again the Lord spoke through T.D. Jakes as I was folding laundry he spoke, "You're the youth pastor at your church and you just found out your son is doing cocaine". I thought my world had crashed! What had we done wrong? What didn't I do right? What guilt, what shame...how could we survive this? I gave my all and this is what I get ...nothing back? That's how it feels, you feel betrayed. You feel guilt you feel remorse for what you could have done different.

You go through this season of darkness and confusion. Did I do enough? Did I do too much? Your friends tell you not to cry to be strong to say the right things and keep believing and everything they say is right, but let me tell you when your baby, His baby is in such darkness your heart break so desperately. The pain is with you always every waking moment.

In this same season my mother was dying of lung cancer which spread to the brain and then to her liver. It was truly the darkest I had ever lived. I know in whom I believe and He was with me always. He helped me fight the warfare many nights waking me up to pray for my baby, His baby's behalf. I am convinced the enemy was trying to take him out early. It was WARFARE!

My battle was nothing compared to what Christ fought on that cross, for me, for us His babies! How sad He must feel when we turn our backs on Him after He poured everything out for us, his babies! There is NO Greater sacrifice. His is the Greatest Love Story. His love is perfect.

I have learned it isn't easy to love like Him. It is a road that sometimes leads to great pain and darkness, but the hope is that in our weakness He swoops down and picks us up and cradles us "HIS Babies" under the shelter of His wing and nurses us back to wholeness and restoration and builds us up so all this love we poured out on our babies, His babies that was spilled into this world was not a waste but a sacrifice.

He reminds us we are not of this world. He reminds us of His blood that was spilled out and reminds us that the price was paid and we HAVE the Victory! We start to heal once we realize that this baby, this creation, His baby, His creation we must lay at the altar and trust that they belong to Him, The Creator.

I must realize I was only a tiny part of the big plan He has for His baby, His creation. I did not like that I had to lay him down at first, after all "I" was put in charge, to nurture, to hold, to grow, to teach and now I have to give him back? It didn't make sense, that was "my job" being a Mother. It was a hard.

My baby is now healed, whole and completely off drugs. However, I could not do this for him. The only thing I could do for him was completely give him up and give him back to God and let Him heal my son.

I believe the greatest love any parent can give is the sacrifice of giving your child back to their creator, surrendering control and letting go.

5

Expectations

By Michelle Thompson-Davis

When the nurse walked into my little exam room, I couldn't believe it when she told me that the test was positive. I was 22, about to start my senior year of college, and alone.

"Was I really pregnant?" I asked myself.

I couldn't believe that I was pregnant. I was a believer and had strived to live my life according to His word.

"I had only sinned a little compared with some of my friends", I thought. "How could this have happened?"

Well, I knew how it had happened; I just couldn't believe that it was happening to me. I did not plan on having sex with my ex-boyfriend. We had been over for 4 months, but I was drinking and believing every word that came out of his mouth. I wanted it to be true. I wanted to be loved by him.

Being pregnant is an unseen condition, at least in its early stages. Why would I trust some stupid test that used urine to determine the state of pregnancy? I wanted to believe that she was just lying. The smug nurse was just trying to lord my sin over me. She was just being cruel with her eyes and smirk as she asked me if I was going to keep it or have an abortion.

"What? What did she say to me? Was I going to have an abortion of a baby that I didn't believe that I was pregnant with?"

I walked out of the little room in shock. The test turned out to be positive. I wasn't going to get married; I had just heard a couple days before that my handsome prince-turned-"Frog" was living with another woman. I offered him my heart, and he lied to me. I allowed him to use me. I felt alone, heartbroken, and used, and the test was positive.

If the test is positive, then I must be pregnant even though I can't see any proof. I have to believe that I'm pregnant without further evidence. I hadn't seen the test results. I should have demanded she show me the evidence.

"What am I going to do? My life is ruined. I need a plan."

All of my thoughts just swirled around my brain like tornadoes in a wild Texas thunderstorm. Then it hit me, "I love my baby. I'm pregnant, and while I may pay the wage of my sin forever. I am still going to love this baby even if I do it all on my own."

But I didn't have to do it all on my own. I had my savior who forgave my sins even though I did not. Riddled with guilt I persecuted myself in spite of the circle of amazing, loving friends God always sent at my lowest moments. He loves me like that. He loves you like that. He was going to love my baby like that.

About the third month of my pregnancy, I was deep into the deception of having to conceal my pregnant state during student teaching when I felt the first little flutter of a movement. I thought maybe I had eaten something wrong, but it was a flutter. That flutter was the first real evidence that I wasn't just getting fat, that the nurse had not been deceiving me. Sometimes, in my moments of grief, I would just focus all of my energy and love on that flutter of hope for a new beginning, wanting to believe that hope would come yet so afraid that it wouldn't.

Regardless of the circumstance, I was going to be the mom that I didn't have. I wasn't going to be haunted by my past and let my stupidity, willfulness, shame, guilt and sin ruin my child's life. I knew that the absence of a father would be enough of a crutch for her; I didn't want her mom not finishing school to be another. I became very determined; giving up was not an option with Christ.

There were so many nights that I laid in bed achingly alone, sorry for my unborn child, and so desperately disappointed in love. I cried myself to sleep under the gravity of my circumstances rocking back and forth in my savior's arms. I had broken a personal promise to not have sex before marriage and to never have a child go through a broken home. I had to make this right; I was going to fix this.

Jesus held me and whispered, "You are not alone."

Sonogram evidence, right in front of me on the screen was this bizarre, peanut shaped thing with limbs growing in my belly. It moved on the screen, and I felt it. I knew that I was absolutely pregnant. I knew that I was really going to have a baby, and she needed me to get myself straight. She needed me to pull it together. She needed me to get over myself, my broken heart, my sin, my grief, and my remorse. She needed me to accept forgiveness and to fully accept grace.

I asked Jesus for a do-over and sought His will again. Two of my best friends became my birth partners; they helped through the whole pregnancy until I went to live with my dad for the last trimester. I graduated with my bachelors in December of '94. I was determined to make it. My baby girl was due in April. By the size of my belly, the amazing moving of little body parts across my torso that could be seen pushing my skin, there was no denying the growth of life and promise inside of me.

As April approached, I prepared. My family threw me a shower, regardless of my circumstances and shame, which meant so much to me. I began collecting clothes, furniture, bottles, and all of those special little baby items that help you feel prepared. I started to have those little preparation pains about a month before she was due. Excitement built, I knew that she was ready to come. I was picking out names for her and so was her dad. He was, at the least, willing to be a part of her life. (He loved her; he just didn't love me. Such is life in your own will.)

When induction day came, I was over the moon with joy. I was packed, organized and prepared. Everything was ready and in its place. I was ready. After hours of labor, I gave birth to the most beautiful little girl. IT wasn't a lie; there really was a life growing inside of me. The evidence was true. The pain was brutal, but the baby was so worth it. As soon as I held her in my arms, I had no memory of the pain that I had just gone through. None of the pain, hurt, or heartbreak mattered anymore.

I loved her even more the moment that I saw her. I never wanted to put her down. I poured all the love I could into her. I never let her cry, and sometimes still struggle with not wanting her to ever cry today. I love her with everything that I have to give through Christ. She is a blessing that came out of the ashes of a broken, sin filled choice. I chose life, and I have been blessed. There has been a wage to my sin, but the joy so overshadows it. God is good. God delivers His promises.

Today, my daughter is United States Navy member of the Ceremonial Guard. She is serving her country, and she may have the opportunity in the next 2 years to serve at the inauguration of a new president or funeral for one of our past presidents or servicemen.

Regardless of the circumstances and pain, I have a beautiful strong daughter and an amazing life. I have given God my broken, ashy life, and He gives me a promise that I want with every ounce of my being, spirit, mind, and soul. I want His will and His promise so badly that I can feel it, see it, taste it...I see the vision. I see the movement across my plane of existence, and I can't wait for the Master's next earthly delivery for me. I am preparing. I am ready. I am overcome with expectancy.

"I tell you the truth; you will weep and mourn while the world rejoices. You will grieve, but your grief will turn to joy. A woman giving birth to a child has pain because her time has come; but when her baby is born she forgets the anguish because of her joy that a child is born into the world. So with you: now is your time of grief, but I will see you again and you will rejoice, and no one will take away your joy. In that day you will no longer ask me anything. I tell you the truth, my Father will give you whatever you ask in my name. Until now you have not asked for anything in my name. Ask and you will receive, and your joy will be complete." John 16: 20-24

> Please visit Michele's blog;
>
> InHisTrenches@blogspot.com
>
> *She is currently working on publishing two books Positude and In His Trenches.*

Oh, Sweet,

She is how old?

She does not look it". "I hope I'll look that good".

Autumn; Beautiful tan, brown, reds and orange.

Cool breezes early in the morning as you spend time

in a loving relationship with your God you have

grown to know so intimately.

You are Autumn!

He smiles down on his creation that He has watched grow from

spring to summer and now, a woman.

A true woman of God;

You are Autumn.

You confidence is bold and revealing. Your incredible fall

colors are a telling sign of an incredible journey

from spring to summer and here you are.

You have arrived.

You open your loving branches and welcome the birds of

summer and the squirrels of spring to come and rest a while.

Oh your beauty. Spring and summer sit and dream that

someday………………………………

Winter

Philippians 4:8-9

Whatever is true, whatever is noble, whatever is right, whatever is pure, whatever is lovely, whatever is admirable-if anything is excellent or praiseworthy-think about such things.

What is the true winter season in our lives? Is it wrinkles and gray hair mixed with long awaited visits in a nursing home? Is it your grandchildren having children, making you a great grandparent that is talked about fondly with reverence and respect? Or is it a dark place that you have walked through or survived where you feel stronger than you ever thought that you were for surviving and actually growing through the experience?

Winter encompasses all of these things. The title is earned through age, experience and a life well lived. It is beautiful white hair sitting on a wrinkled thin face. It is holding on tight in a dark moment waiting for the light to shine, warm your face and ease your pain. Its closure to a long journey, which was a wild ride you had never imagined.

You don't have to be a certain age to experience a winter season, and you will most likely experience several winters on your journey until you actually resemble winter in your face, hair, hands and skin. No matter which winter it may be, it is beauty beyond any compare, it is majestic, it is respected and it is earned.

1

Margaret

Margaret would stand about 5 feet tall if she stood straight, but she hunches over severely and this makes her about 4"10 on a good day. I don't know Margaret's age and have never been comfortable enough to ask, not to mention she is extremely hard of hearing, so I always try to keep my questions to the bare minimum, for example; "Margaret, would you like your usual roll and coffee?"

She always answers, "hmmmh", which means yes, and I serve her a cinnamon roll and a small black coffee with half coffee and half water in the cup.

Margaret walks to the coffee shop when she comes, which is usually a couple of times a week. Margaret walks everywhere she travels. I don't think it is because she cannot drive as much as it is that she does not have a vehicle to drive.

Margaret was born and raised in Schulenburg. I asked her once how high school was when she went here and she told me that she never went to high school. Margaret was a poor country girl and had to drop out of school in the fourth grade to help her family work the farm.

This was common for small town life when Margaret was growing up. People had to do what they had to do to survive, including using their young children for labor.

Margaret is still hard working even in her golden years. I hate to guess for fear that I might be wrong, but I assume, safely or not, that Margaret is in her late 70's or early 80's. She cleans for a living. I guess it is homes that she cleans, or perhaps offices, but I'm not really sure. I do know, you might see Margaret walking around town on any given day, on her usual route, which is to her job, wherever she may be cleaning that day, the local bar or the shop downtown if it is early enough for coffee and too early for beer.

Margaret rarely smiles and you would most likely see her small hunched over frame with a serious scowl on her face than any other expression. Except for when Bert, a 6'4" 300 lb. local pastor, comes in The Shop for a visit, and offers to buy her a cinnamon roll and coffee. This always makes Margaret light up and smile. It's a delight to see someone illuminated, which has spent most of her days shadowed, over the kindness of a gentle giant named Bert.

2

Tears from Heaven

My life is pretty normal. I have two grown daughters, and several grandchildren, all making me extremely proud. My husband is my best friend and I have what I would call a good, seemingly normal life in a wonderful small town where things just roll with ease: most of the time.

However, my seemingly normal life came to an end the day I received the call that my precious mother had begun a downward spiral in her health. My Mother suffered with acid reflux and mild depression. She was an amazing woman, the most amazing resilient women I had ever known.

My Father had not been the best husband to this lovely woman. He was an alcoholic and struggled with anger issues. He passed several years back and my Mom was known as the glue that held us all together and the constant rock in all of our lives.

There was not any amount of medicine that could help relieve the pain she experienced from the reflux. She wanted desperately to eat and drink for us kids, just like she had spent her entire life, enduring for her children, but nothing seemed to agree with her stomach. I, the oldest of four children, had been my Mothers caregiver for the last three years, along with the help from the nursing center where she was a resident.

The day that my Mother had decided to completely quit eating and drinking was the day that my normal life, became very abnormal. I began to go to the nursing center religiously three times a day. Each time I would hope, pray, encourage and then try to force my Mom to eat or drink something.

I could not understand why she was refusing something so vital to life such as food and water. I knew that if I could not convince her to begin eating and drinking, that she would eventually give up on her life, if she hadn't already. I was frustrated, afraid and nowhere near ready to accept losing my Mother. My life could not work without my Mother.

She was my constant, my wisdom, my winter and this autumn baby was not ready to take her place.

I would come home from the center drained and exhausted from trying to convince my Mother to eat. She would begin to try, to please me and make me happy, but at the end, would always push it away and gently turn her head with tears in her eyes.

"How does someone choose not to eat and why", I would cry out to God in my exasperation.

Every day, for three weeks I and my younger siblings would talk to her, plead with her and beg her to eat.

"Please mommy, please just a little and we promise we will leave you alone", I would say softly.

"I'll try", she would respond each morning.

However, she never ate a bite.

"I'll try", she said at lunch.

Yet, she would have nothing to eat or drink.

"I'll try", again at dinner.

Still, she would turn her head with tears in her sweet eyes and nothing.

We knew that she was declining in her health and that it was appropriate timing to call hospice in to help us all through this process. Her weight was rapidly dropping and she could no longer hold her body up on her own.

She began to speak less and less and eventually could barely speak to all. I could feel my Mother slipping away from me little by little each day. I was angry with her and was troubled with trying to understand why she would no longer want to live. I felt like she was choosing to die.

She was not sick, no major illness to be concerned with. She just stopped eating, just as simple as that. She just seemed to not want to live anymore. She was done, and at first, I could not understand why.

"Please fight Mother, please", I would say to her in an accretive, strong voice!

Then, one day as I kept faithful vigil by her side, the Lord spoke to my heart.

"I am sufficient for all your needs"

Oh, how I needed to hear those words from my Father. You see, when our parents are leaving this world it is so very hard for us because they are our nurturers, our caregivers and our connection to life. The Lords words comforted my heart that day and told me that even though my Mother would soon be leaving this Earth, I would not be left alone. I would still have my heavenly Father to nurture and care for me. I could always run into his arms.

As Mother's days began to draw to a close, I began to experience a peace that transcends understanding. I had a peace that came from my heavenly Father and a new understanding of how all the seasons in our lives eventually change and end.

I would sit by her bed, rub her hands, comb her hair, sing some of her favorite songs or play her favorite gospel CD for her and just rest and listen along with Mother. It was a wonderful time and I began to let go of my frustration and control and just sit as one with my Mommy. It was spiritual, beautiful and a complete blessing from God.

On Wednesday, August 29th, my new abnormal life was normal. I would go see Mother in the morning, go run errands, go back to see her in the afternoon, and then again in evening. I left her bedside at 11:19 a.m. and told her that I would be back soon and I loved her. However, shortly after I drove away, my heart stirred and I knew that I must get back to my Mother.

I quickly walked back into her room, kissed her forehead and told her I was back. She made her usual grunt to let me know that she understood. Something in my heart told me that I must tell my Mother that it is ok with me if she wants to go. I prayed for God to grant me the strength.

I said, "just rest Mom, go on now and see nana and; (my brother), it's ok".

My niece was scheduled to arrive soon to stay with Mom and I was going to go. However, I could not take my eyes off my Mother. I knew I should not leave. She had never looked more beautiful or strong.

Her white hair glistened with majesty and she was so serene. Her skin was flawless and I stroked her tiny long fingers that had tirelessly prepared so many meals for me. She folded her arms across her chest, took a deep breath and left for her heavenly home.

That morning of my Mother's passing, I had written in my journal, "Lord, you know that my Mother is uncomfortable and in pain, please take her home soon to be with you so she can rest in a new body with no more hurts".

I thank God for embracing my Mother and welcoming her to His home that day. The time of my Mothers passing was 6:10 p.m., when I felt the beautiful tears from heaven.

3

Listen close, you will find wisdom

Nancy holds herself like a queen, because she is a queen. She is regal in every way. She is always seen completely put together in a long flowing skirt and a large beautiful hat sitting on top of her head with her hair pulled up and every strand in place. I have never seen Nancy wear any makeup and her strong soft face and perfect lips do not need anything to enhance them.

She is well in her seventies and speaks slowly and directly with perfect diction. The attention of everyone stops and is drawn to her when she walks in the room, it is not by demand, but by her deserving air and spirit.

Nancy loves to talk and share her wisdom. She is strong, knowledgeable, and spent many years teaching etiquette lessons overseas. She is the epitome of class and sophistication, but does not put on any airs and is humble in spirit and gentle. Nancy only loves one thing more than people, and that is helping those people she loves.

She is one of those people that if she had only five dollars left to her name, and you needed five dollars, then the five dollars would be yours, without a second thought.

Nancy is a cancer survivor and has received the beautiful gift that cancer can bring into our lives. She has an outlook that most people will never experience, an appreciation for people and the human spirit. She views her life as a gift and lives each day to discover new ways that she can return the gift she has been given to the world.

I sat with Nancy that quiet afternoon and was attempting to write her story, however, as I began listening to her speak, which is all too easy to do, I began to just write what Nancy shared. I felt led to write and simply share her thoughts, and if you listen closely to what she says, you will find wisdom. This is what Nancy shared with me on the quite afternoon;

"You're at MD Anderson and you look around and see that everyone around you has their toes on the line, because they just may not make it. All of your stuff, all of the things that you think are so important to you, and suddenly you realize that we perish each alone and no one or nothing can be with you. You become more aware of this as you watch friends and family pass and you can get to a point that there is no fear in it."

"I don't want to say that I would look forward to it, but I would like to say that as you become more in proximity to that age group, expressing yourself truly becomes easier. My dad use to say that it is so much easier passing the age of 65 because people are much more accepting to you expressing yourself. I feel that as I get older, I have more grace from people and perhaps it is because as we age and those around us age, we begin to remind many people of someone that they love, or perhaps they lost. "

"There was a beautiful, wise, older, black lady I knew……."

She would always tell me, "Leave it be, leave it be. You just need to give it a little time and most things will eventually level off."

"When people have a different background, or are different from us and we criticize that, then we are criticizing what God has created. If you poke at someone or ridicule them, then you are ridiculing what God has made and in fact ridiculing God. "

"I grew up in a time when we had an inbred fear of people that are different from us. It is a lot of learned behavior. We have learned from other generations. People stop teaching their generations how to care for each other, and then it gets lost. "

"When we forget how to encourage and care for people then that ability ceases to exist. How will we know how? To do a kind deed, or say a kind word is far better than any gift, and a wise man knows how to give both.

"Everything is learned behavior. My daughter called me today from the convent in Switzerland and I had not talked to her in a while." She said, "That people are learning this behavior to hate and be angry. "

"People are not going by the 10 commandments anymore, they are thinking of them as the 10 suggestions. Well, they are not the 10 suggestions, they are in fact the 10 commandments and this is where we are going wrong. What has happened to the family tree? It is no longer the family tree, it is the family vine, and it is not the child's fault. "

"Nothing seems to be in order anymore. People are giving themselves excuses to be untruthful. They are irrationally rationalizing permission to commit acts of permanent damage to innocent victims. They have no intentions of admitting guilt or admitting wrong. "

"When you have come to a point that you ignore the innocence of someone that you are supposed to be helping protect, and you override that duty, in your own choosing and own rational, and you use the basic human right to gratify your compulsion or your own self, then society has failed. This is about choices. Our society is giving permission to devour the innocent at the expense of others."

"Now, I will close with a memory of when my children were young. We always did well and had more than enough. My husband was a lawyer and successful. However, in all my memories of Christmas, the best gift my children ever received at Christmas was the year that our family had fallen on hard times and did not have any money to buy presents."

We were all given the amazing gift that year of celebrating our Saviors birth and realizing the true meaning of Christmas. Now that was the best Christmas of my life!

4

The Gift

    I awoke, far before the sun around 5:00 a.m. I journeyed out the back porch of the cabin and snuggled down in a blanket. There was one other lady up; Oh, how I long to remember her name. I close my eyes and can see her beautiful, soft, face, mapped out with lines of laughter, tears and a life well lived. She was the epitome of Winter, yet my new beginning, my Spring! This Beautiful woman compassed Spring, Summer, Autumn and Winter, she was the journey and she was glistening.

    She bent around the corner and handed me a cup of coffee, smiled and gently said,

"I know we may all seem old to you young ones, but were all on the same journey".

    She then, drifted off like the snow and that's when God gave me Seasons. I sat there that cool morning just writing as fast as I could. It was like He was pouring the words into me, and they were overflowing out faster than I could catch them with my pen. It was fun and it was easy. It was one of those moments in life that everything felt perfect and right in my world. I was writing for the Lord and the joy and peace was indescribable.

As soon as I wrote the last word, that same sweet, beautiful lady with hair as white as the snow came back around the corner and asked,

"What are you writing"?

I said, "Will you sit with me and let me read it to you"?

She smiled warmly and snuggled down beside me on that beautiful chilly fall morning as the sun was now about to show it's warm face above the horizon. I sat there with Winter and read Seasons to her. When I was finished, she looked at me and asked,

"What are you going to do with that poem"?

"I don't know", I said, "probably nothing, why"?

She looked at me straight in the eyes and in an assertive, raspy, strong voice, she said,

"God has given you a gift and if you do not share this gift and give it back to the world, this would be a sin".

She stopped sighed and said," You have to give back what God has given to you'.

I just sat there looking at her.

"Do you hear me young lady"?

That night I prayed and asked the Lord, "Lord, what do I do?" He replied!

"Write down what I put in your heart and make it plain on paper, so that a herald may run with it. Then wait, I will use it at an appointed time." Habakkuk 2:1

BEAUTY BEYOND COMPARE!

Your white winter snow glistens with majesty.

You cover the Earth, standing tall above the

Spring, Summer and Fall, that long to have you

wrap your arms around them and hold them tight.

You speak a bit slower, and it is needed.

Your voice demands attention.

We listen a little closer......

Of all the seasons, you radiate the most beauty.

You glisten.

Your wisdom is so needed.

Your walk and relationship with the Lord is like a lake that is frozen solid. Spring, Summer and Autumn come and skate across your surface, or cut a hole and go deep beneath to fish for food and nourishment.

Oh Winter,

solid, strong, bold..................glistening

Winter.

About The Author:

Christine Heinrich is the mother of two daughters and lives in the small rural town of Schulenburg, Texas where she owns and runs a coffee shop and writes. She is the originator of Seasons and has written the majority of the stories in this project, with the exception of, **My Baby, His Baby; Expectations and Jack**.

However the original author of these three pieces is dually noted after each story. The stories in Seasons, are either inspired or created by Christine Heinrich, or are true stories shared by real people the Author has asked specifically to share their story. Christine Heinrich has written, or has re-written these stories to share in the book "Seasons".

Christine Heinrich graduated with a bachelor degree in Theatre and English and loves to write poetry and about people and their stories. Christine believes everyone has a story in their heart and it should be shared to inspire and help one another.

Please be encouraged to read this book together with a group and discuss openly how each individual may relate to certain stories shared in this project. The Author's desire is that this project will inspire those reading to share their stories with one another and realize, as we heal and grow through the seasons in our lives, we all have a story.

The Project

You are amazing and we all need to hear your story. In 2009, I was on a plane coming back from a writer's conference when God placed it on my heart to turn my poem Seasons into a compilation of women's stories in a book titled Seasons...The Project.

This is more than just one book of stories, it is a series of stories that women need to share with one another. However, I need your stories about the seasons you have experienced in your own lives to make this project a success.

I have prayed that God would bring just the right women across my path to be a part of the Seasons project and series, and if you are reading this now and feel you have something to share with the women of this world, than you are one of the ones that He has chosen to take part of this journey with me, and reach women everywhere.

Would you be willing to take part of this project by sharing your story in the second compilation book seasons 2?

You are invited to share your story with me. You don't have to be a writer, or even a story teller to share. God will help me share your story; all you have to be is willing. Please contact me at

cgalipp@gmail.com

Your Story

Thank you Lord, for giving me Seasons.

Thank you for Spring;

Thank you for Summer;

Thank you for Autumn;

And most importantly,

Thank you for Winter!

May we never forget the Seasons in our lives, may we always love, support and encourage one another through our journeys. I love you My Dear Heavenly Father and Most Importantly Thank you for my gifts may they forever be used to bring you glory.

Made in the USA
San Bernardino, CA
21 April 2015